I0605231

MISSION: SPACE SCIENCE

ASTEROIDS AND COMETS

Published in 2025 by **Cheriton Children's Books**
1 Bank Drive West, Shrewsbury, Shropshire, SY3 9DJ

First Edition

Author: Sarah Eason
Designers: Paul Myerscough and Steve Mead
Editor: Jennifer Sanderson
Proofreader: Ella Newby
Consultant: David Hawksett, BSc

Picture credits: Cover: Shutterstock/Sergey Nivens (t), Shutterstock/Vadim Sadovski (b). Inside: p4b: Shutterstock/Diane Kulpinski, p4t: Shutterstock/Elena Schweitzer, p6b: Wikimedia Commons/Internet Archive Book Images, p6t: Wikimedia Commons/James St. John, p7: Shutterstock/BTC Studio, p8: Wikimedia Commons/Myrabella, p9: ESO/Y. Beletsky, p10: Shutterstock/Triff, p11b: Wikimedia Commons/Godfrey Kneller, p11t: Wikimedia Commons/Hans Bernhard, p12: Wikimedia Commons/National Museum of the U.S. Navy, p13b: Shutterstock/Darkdiamond67, p13t: NASA, p14: NASA/JPL-Caltech/LMSS, p15: NASA, p16: NASA/JPL-Caltech/UMD/Pat Rawlings, p17: Wikimedia Commons/DLR, p18: Shutterstock/Buradaki, p19b: NASA/JPL-Caltech/UCLA, p19t: Shutterstock/24K-Production, p20: NASA, p21b: Shutterstock/Elena11, p21t: ISAS/JAXA, p22: NASA/IAU, p23: NASA/GSFC, pp24-25: Shutterstock/Hamara, p24b: Shutterstock/Warpaint, p25: NASA/JPL-Caltech/University of Arizona, p26: Shutterstock/Geermy, p27b: Shutterstock/Vadim Sadovski, p27t: Shutterstock/Galyna Andrushko, p28: Wikimedia Commons/Konstantin Kudinov, p29b: Shutterstock/Buradaki, p29t: Shutterstock/Framalicious, p30: Shutterstock/Alex K Photography, p31: Shutterstock/Artsiom P, p32: Shutterstock/Serrgey75, p33b: NASA/JPL-Caltech, p33t: Shutterstock/Nazarii Neshcherenskyi, p34: NASA/Johns Hopkins University Applied Physics Laboratory/Southwest Research Institute, p35: NASA/ESA/Caltech/M. Brown, p36: NASA/ESA/A. Schaller, p37: Wikimedia Commons/Kevin M. Gill, p38: Wikimedia Commons/George E. Koronaios, p39: Shutterstock/Elzloy, p40: NASA, p41: NASA/JPL-Caltech, p42b: NASA/JPL-Caltech/ASU, p42t: Shutterstock/Dotted Yeti, p43: Shutterstock/Raymond Cassel, p44: NASA/Ben Smegelsky, p45: Shutterstock/Gorodenkoff.

Printed in China

CONTENTS

Chapter 1

OUR SECRET SOLAR SYSTEM

Think of the solar system, and what do you picture? There is the sun at the center, of course, shining brightly. Surrounding it are Earth and the other seven planets, each orbiting the sun on its own path. Is that it? You may have heard about Pluto, whose orbit crosses that of Neptune and used to be considered a planet but is now classified as a dwarf planet. But what else could there be in our solar system?

Trillions of Objects

It turns out that there is a lot more to the solar system than just a star and eight planets. The solar system includes everything that is held in orbit by the sun's gravity. Excluding the sun, the planets are the biggest objects in the solar system but there are trillions of smaller objects too. These include nearly 300 moons orbiting the planets, five recognized dwarf planets, and more than 150 million asteroids.

Comets and asteroids shoot across the night sky in a spectacular display.

At the very center of our solar system is a dazzling ball of energy—our sun.

Scratching the Surface

However, even that is only scratching the surface. Comets swoop in from the outer reaches of the solar system, making a long loop around the sun before disappearing back to where they came from. A largely unexplored region called the Kuiper Belt lies outside the orbit of Neptune and is home to trillions of objects. Many of them are probably big enough to be classified as dwarf planets, once more is known about them. Then there are also the centaurs and trojans. Centaurs are small solar system bodies that are similar in size to asteroids. They are mainly found between Jupiter and Neptune. A trojan is a space body that shares an orbit with a planet or moon.

YOUR MISSION

In this book we will explore asteroids and comets in detail, looking at what we know about them and how we learned it. You will also be given thought-provoking space missions to complete that will draw on:

- Your STEM skills: these are science, technology, engineering, and math skills.
- Your social skills: these include identifying skills and strengths in others, team building, persuasive skills, and learning how to work collaboratively.
- Your critical thinking skills: these include being able to evaluate and analyze information, think independently about problems and find solutions, and draw your own conclusions.

All the above skills are vital for successful space exploration—ask any space scientist! So, are you mission-ready? Let's begin the missions and find out.

SPACE SCIENCE

The solar system goes much farther than the most outlying planet, Neptune, but just how big it is depends on how you define it. The heliopause marks the boundary of the heliosphere, an area filled with solar magnetic fields and solar winds. However, beyond that is the Oort Cloud, an enormous collection of icy comets. They are outside the heliosphere but still affected by the sun's gravity, so they are usually considered to be part of the solar system.

People Who Studied the Skies

Long before telescopes were invented, people studied the skies. They tracked the movements of the sun, moon, and stars, as well as those planets that could be seen with the naked eye: Mercury, Venus, Mars, Jupiter, and Saturn. Although the planets look a lot like stars when seen from Earth, early astronomers could tell that they were different because of the movements they made over the course of a year.

This Roman coin shows a comet. Like many other ancient civilizations, the Romans were fascinated by the night sky and the mysterious objects in it.

Before Modern Times

Before electric light affected our view of the skies, there would have been thousands of stars visible on a clear night. However, most of the other objects in the solar system are too small or too far away to be seen without a telescope. Moons circling other planets, asteroids, and Kuiper Belt objects (KBOs) were completely unknown to ancient peoples.

This drawing shows "shooting stars" (see opposite) in the sky above an ocean with a ship at sail. The image was made by an English sailor in the 1800s.

Showing up from Time to Time

However, a few of our solar system neighbors did make appearances from time to time, and when they showed up, they really made a splash! When some comets approach Earth on their way to the sun, they can be seen moving brightly across the sky, their long tails streaming out behind them. Many people interpreted comets as a sign that something bad would happen soon: the death of a king, war, or natural disaster, for example.

Shooting Stars

The other objects that were often seen were meteors, sometimes called "shooting stars." These are much more common than comets, and if you happen to be looking in the right place at the right time, you can see one most nights. Sometimes, they come in groups, called a meteor shower, and many people thought they brought good luck. One culture believed that seeing one meteor would bring good fortune, but three in one night would bring a sign that something bad would happen soon.

SPACE HISTORY

Meteors sometimes fall to Earth in the form of stones that we call meteorites. For thousands of years, people have found and collected them. They must have seen some of them fall from the sky, an experience that would have been both mysterious and terrifying. Many meteorites have been found in contexts that suggest that they were worshiped or believed to have special powers.

In ancient times, people often believed that a meteor shower meant misfortune and disaster were on their way.

Studying the Data

By the eighteenth century, there was enough data for astronomers and mathematicians to study patterns in comets. In 1705, Edmond Halley (1656–1742) analyzed historical sightings of 23 different comets, according to Newton's Laws of Motion. He noticed that three of them (from 1531, 1607, and 1682) had very similar paths. He theorized that they must have all been the same comet, and predicted that it would return in 1758 or 1759. He was right! The comet is now called Halley's Comet in his honor.

The famous Bayeaux Tapestry records the 1066 Norman invasion of England, and the sighting of Halley's Comet.

A Solar System Revolution

During the eighteenth century, telescopes were revolutionizing the study of the solar system. Some mathematicians noticed that the distance of the planets from the sun seemed to form a pattern. As you move out from Mercury, the gap between the planets increases at a regular rate. The six known planets fit this pattern very neatly, with one exception: there was a huge gap between Mars and Jupiter, with just the right amount of space for a missing planet in between. When Uranus was discovered in 1781, it also fit neatly into the pattern, encouraging scientists to believe that there really was a planet between Mars and Jupiter!

Space Science

The pattern of planets in relation to the sun was called Bode's Law, and most scientists now believe that it is just a coincidence, rather than a law of nature. When Neptune was discovered in 1846, its position went against Bode's Law. After years of searching, astronomers concluded that there was no large planet between Mars and Jupiter.

This photograph shows Jupiter, Venus, and Mercury in the sky above the La Silia Observatory in Chile, South America.

Searching for the Missing Planet

By the end of the century, a group of astronomers had formed a team to search for the missing planet using an observatory in Germany, and named themselves the "Celestial Police." Italian astronomer, Giuseppe Piazzi (1746–1826), thought he beat them to it when he discovered Ceres in 1801. Piazzi and other scientists considered it a planet, however, Ceres was fewer than 600 miles (966 km) across—even the smallest planet, Mercury, is more than 3,000 miles (4,828 km) across. After half a century of "planet" status, during which other objects even smaller than Ceres were discovered, Ceres was reclassified as an asteroid.

YOUR MISSION

We have only just begun to explore and understand space. Imagine it is your task to plan a space mission to discover other unusual bodies in space. In your planning, consider:

- Goals and objectives: what would you want to achieve?
- Equipment: what tools and devices might be employed?
- Transportation: what factors need to be considered?
- Funding and investment: how would you secure this?

Chapter 2

SPECTACULAR COMETS

Comets have inspired many fantastic stories and legends, but the truth behind them is fairly simple. They are small, icy objects, mostly between 6 and 25 miles (9.7 and 40 km) in diameter, and they heat up when they pass close to the sun. When this happens, some of a comet's icy center (called the nucleus) turns to gas, forming a thin atmosphere called a coma. The solar wind blows the coma material, which makes a comet's trademark tails. A comet's tails stream out for millions of miles.

Icy Lumps in the Sky

Comets are found in the outer reaches of the solar system, in the Kuiper Belt, and the Oort Cloud. Many of these icy lumps will never leave their home, but others have their orbits disturbed (usually by the gravity of another object) and are sent on a new path. Those that move toward the sun begin to vaporize in the warmer areas of the inner solar system, which creates the coma and tails.

Comets can be identified by the long tails that stretch behind them as the spectacular objects streak through the sky.

Not a Round Orbit

Unlike planets, comets traveling around the sun do not follow a round orbit. Instead, they travel in very long, thin loops. Once they pass the sun they do not continue across to the other side of the solar system; instead, they loop back around and return to where they came from. Short-period comets, like Halley's Comet, mainly come from the Kuiper Belt and complete an orbit in fewer than 200 years. Long-period comets come from the Oort Cloud and can take 30 million years to make a trip around the sun!

This is the spectacular comet Hale-Bopp, which was discovered in the 1990s. It is the brightest comet ever recorded.

SPACE SCIENCE

In the seventeenth century, Sir Isaac Newton (1643–1727), shown right, theorized that the tails of comets were streams of vapor emitted by their bodies and ignited by the sun. In the next century, Immanuel Kant (1724–1804) suggested that the comets themselves were made of a substance that vaporized to form the tail. In 1950, Fred Whipple (1906–2004) correctly proposed that comets are mainly icy objects containing some dust and rock, like a dirty snowball.

The Most Famous Comet

Probably the most famous comet is Halley's Comet, a short-period comet that is visible from Earth every 75 to 76 years. It is the first comet that was recognized to be periodic; that is, to have a regularly timed orbit. It is easily seen by the naked eye when it approaches Earth, and its appearances were recorded throughout history, although people at the time did not realize that it was the same comet returning each time.

First Photographed

When Halley's Comet appeared in 1910, the first-ever images of it were taken. Astronomers were also able to take some readings and learn more about what it was made of. On its next appearance in 1986, conditions for viewing it from Earth were very poor: it did not make a very close approach, and light pollution caused by electricity (which was not such a problem in 1910) prevented many people from being able to see it.

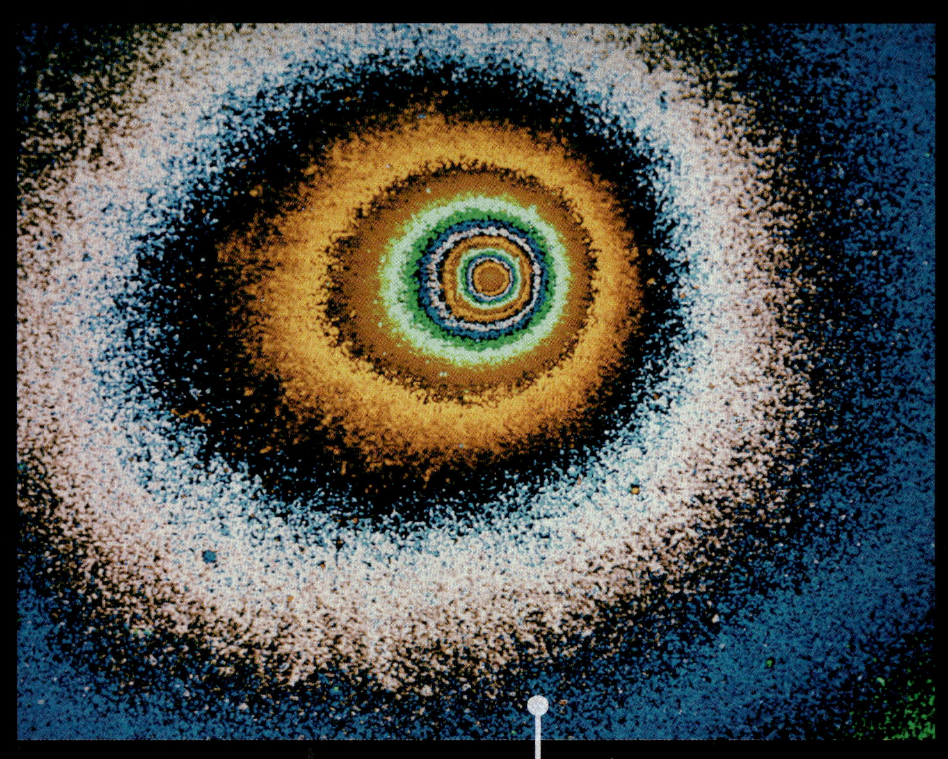

This ultraviolet (UV) image of Halley's Comet shows the circle of gas that surrounds it.

Technology Watch

Despite the poor conditions, scientists were able to use technology to make the most of Halley's approach. A French/Soviet probe sent back the first-ever image of its nucleus. The European Space Agency (ESA) launched the Giotto probe, which made the closest pass to the nucleus and sent back even better images. Two Japanese probes also studied the comet. The International Cometary Explorer (ICE) spacecraft passed through the comet's tail, although it never got particularly close to the comet itself. Two space shuttle missions from the National Aeronautics and Space Administration (NASA) were planned to study the comet, but they were canceled after the Challenger space shuttle exploded in 1986. With improvements in technology, who knows what we might learn when the comet returns in 2061?

The comet Oumuamua is the first object from outer space that has been detected passing through our solar system.

Space History

A Chinese historian recorded a comet as far back as 240 BCE, a year when Halley would have been visible. Archeologists have found records of its next two appearances on Babylonian tablets, and historians from many cultures recorded the next few visits. When it appeared again in 1066, it was seen as an omen that predicted the victory of the Norman king William the Conqueror over the English king.

This image showing Oumuamua approaching our galaxy, the Milky Way, was created by NASA. The comet traveled from outer space and then eventually entered our solar system.

Dark Due to Dust

Giotto found that Halley's nucleus was dark, probably because of a thick layer of dust. The material it was releasing was mainly water, with smaller amounts of carbon monoxide, methane, and ammonia. Studying Halley's Comet in 1986 was just the start, and later probes have increased our knowledge of comets. After studying Halley's Comet, Giotto remained in orbit in hibernation mode for more than four years. It was "woken up" in 1990 to get into position for a meeting with Comet Grigg-Skjellerup (a much older comet) in 1992.

A Test Run

NASA's Deep Space 1 spacecraft was launched in 1998. It was mainly designed as a test run for several new technologies, including an ion drive in place of a traditional rocket engine. However, one of its missions was an encounter with Comet Borrelly. Deep Space 1 was able to send back detailed images of the comet's surface that were much clearer than Giotto's images of Halley's Comet.

This is an artist's image of the space probe Stardust on its approach to comet Tempel 1 (see opposite).

Probing with Stardust

The Stardust probe was launched a year after Deep Space 1, and intercepted comet Wild 2. The probe approached as close as 147 miles (237 km) from the comet's nucleus, taking detailed images. Its most impressive achievement was collecting dust samples from the comet's coma, then returning these samples to Earth for scientists to analyze. The Sample Return Capsule parachuted safely to the ground in Utah on January 16, 2006. Stardust also approached the comet Tempel 1 in 2011.

Space Science

In 1994, scientists had an opportunity to see the death of a comet. Shoemaker-Levy 9 had been discovered in orbit around Jupiter the year before. Comets can be "captured" by the gravity of much larger objects, and this is probably what happened to Shoemaker-Levy 9. It had been torn into pieces by Jupiter's gravity, and from July 16 to July 22, 1994, the fragments of the comet smashed into the planet at about 134,000 miles per hour (215,650 kph).

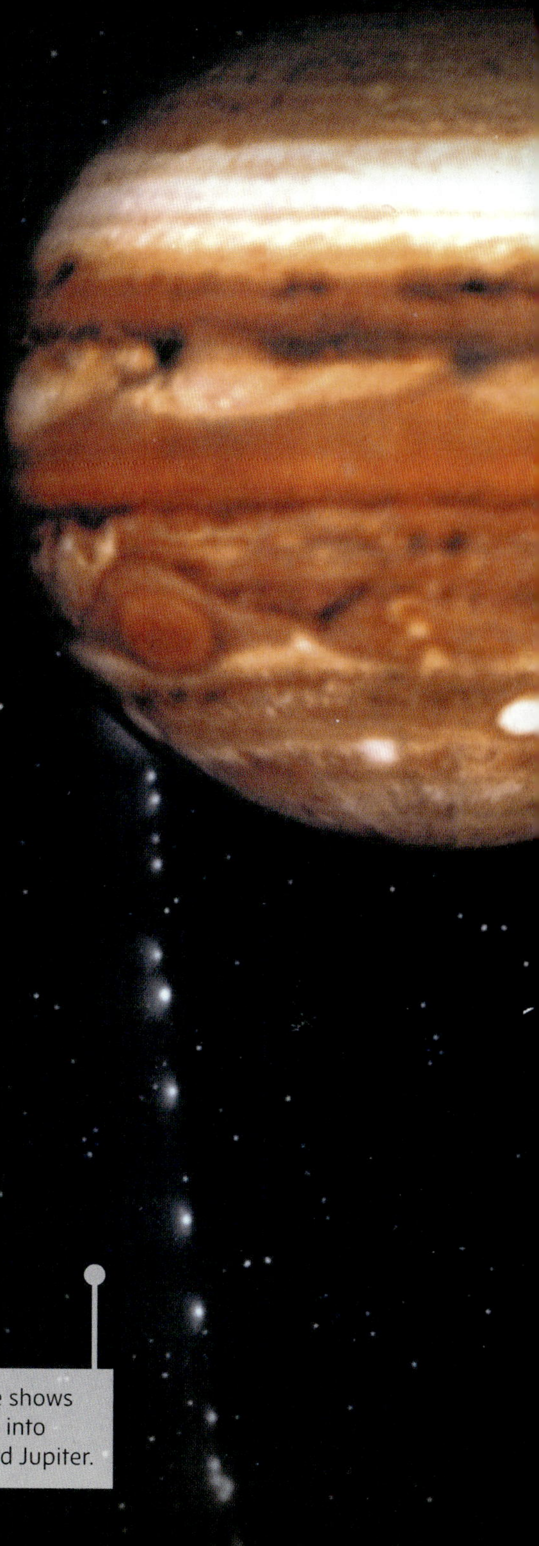

This composite NASA image shows Shoemaker-Levy 9 breaking into fragments on its path toward Jupiter.

A Cloud of Dust and Ice

When the sun first formed, it was surrounded by a flat, disc-shaped cloud made of gas, ice, and dust. As this cloud rotated, the particles in it began to stick together and formed bigger and bigger lumps. Some of the lumps closer to the sun eventually became planets and asteroids, and the ones far from the sun became comets. Astronomers are interested in comets because they are a little like time capsules. Finding out what they are made of can show us what the solar system was like in its very early days.

Mission: Deep Impact

In the 1990s, NASA designed a spacecraft to do just that. The Deep Impact mission was launched in 2005 on a course that would take it to intercept Tempel 1. Unlike previous probes such as Giotto and Stardust, which had only flown past and taken images, Deep Impact would release an impactor. The impactor used its thrusters to move itself into the path of the comet, then crashed into it at a speed of 23,000 miles per hour (37,000 kph). The collision caused a crater 500 feet (152 m) across, and the Deep Impact spacecraft, 300 miles (483 km) away, took images and some other readings. Scientists were surprised to find that the comet contained more dust but less ice than expected.

This artist's image shows the first time Deep Impact encountered the comet Tempel 1 in July 2005.

Rosetta Is Launched

ESA launched Rosetta in 2004 to study the comet Churyumov-Gerasimenko. In 2014, Rosetta successfully entered orbit around the comet. Over the course of its 17-month orbit, it studied the comet in detail, looking for signs of organic compounds—the building blocks of life. This evidence could prove the theory that long ago, comets crashing into Earth "seeded" it with organic molecules.

Philae was designed to touch down on Churyumov-Gerasimenko and fire harpoons to anchor itself firmly to the comet's surface.

Space Science

Rosetta carried a lander called Philae. On November 12, 2014, Philae dropped to comet Churyumov-Gerasimenko's surface. It was a difficult landing, and Philae ended up in an area of deep shadow, which did not receive enough sunlight for its solar panels to recharge its batteries. However, it drilled into the surface and sent back data for more than 50 hours before falling silent.

YOUR MISSION

Imagine it is your task to plan a space mission to land a spacecraft on a comet. In your planning, consider:

- Challenges of the mission: what would they be?
- Solutions to problems: how would you overcome challenges?
- Key STEM skills required to successfully plan and complete the mission: what would they be?

Chapter 3

AMAZING ASTEROIDS

Asteroids are a little like very small planets. The smallest are the size of boulders, and the biggest ones are several hundred miles across. Most of them are found in the asteroid belt that lies between the orbits of Mars and Jupiter. Like comets, they were formed from the "leftovers" in the early days of the solar system. Most of them, especially the smaller ones, are lumpy and oddly shaped. Asteroids are different from comets in several ways. They mostly orbit the sun in a path that is roughly circular, like a planet does, instead of a long, thin loop like a comet's orbit. They are mainly made of rock and metals, although some asteroids are now known to contain water ice. Their surface does not vaporize to give them a coma or a tail.

This artist's image shows the planet Jupiter and the asteroids of the belt that lies between the giant planet and Mars.

Not an Easy Study

The surfaces of asteroids also show craters where other objects have crashed into them. Asteroids may be fairly close to Earth, but studying them is not the easiest job. Most of them are so small that even seen with the powerful Hubble Space Telescope, which can peer into distant galaxies, they appear only as fuzzy blobs. Although we do not have many clear images of asteroids, we have found a lot of asteroids—at least 500,000. Most of them have been found since 1980.

Asteroids are often pitted with the marks of collisions with other space objects. This asteroid, named Psyche, is covered with large craters.

NASA's Wide-field Infrared Survey Explorer (WISE) was launched in 2009. This space telescope was designed to take infrared images of 99 percent of the sky. In its 10-month mission it took more than 1.5 million images—that is one every 11 seconds! It detected more than 4,000 new asteroids. One of its jobs was identifying asteroids orbiting close to Earth.

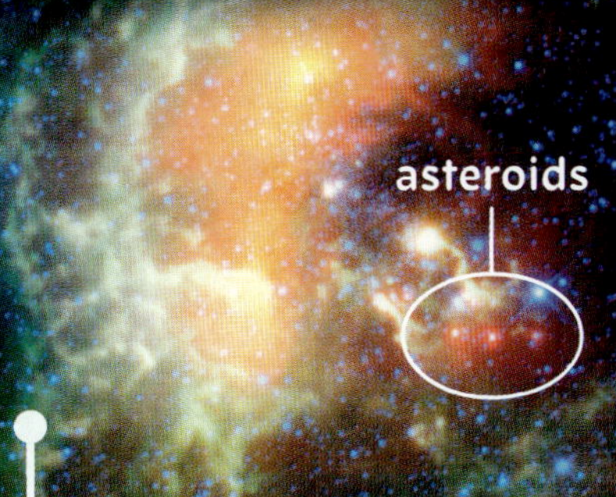

This image taken by WISE shows the Tadpole nebula and asteroids that are passing by it. The asteroids are the red objects in the image.

Space Science

Not all asteroids are found in the asteroid belt. A particular type of asteroid, called a trojan, shares its orbit with a larger object, such as a planet. Trojans stay far enough away from the larger object to avoid crashing into it. There are two large clusters of trojans in the orbit of Jupiter, which were the first to be found. Since then, trojans have been found sharing the orbits of Mars, Neptune, Uranus, two of Saturn's moons, and even Earth.

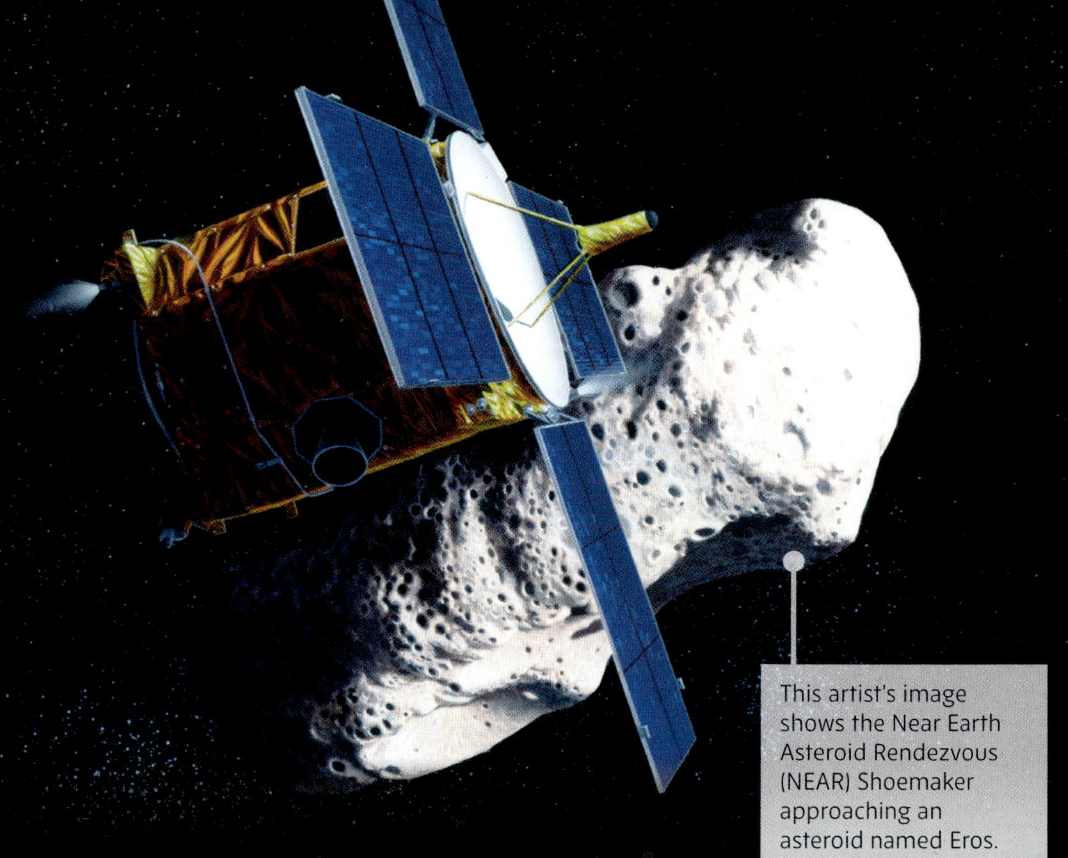

This artist's image shows the Near Earth Asteroid Rendezvous (NEAR) Shoemaker approaching an asteroid named Eros.

Calculated Guesses

We cannot see asteroids clearly through telescopes but we can still learn a little about what they are like. By studying the variation in an asteroid's brightness as it rotates, astronomers can make educated guesses about its shape. Its size can be estimated by measuring how much a star's light dims when an asteroid passes directly in front of it. However, the best way to study asteroids up close is to visit them.

Launched to Study

Several space probes have been launched to study asteroids. The first probe to do an asteroid flyby was Galileo in 1991, on its way to study Jupiter. It took images of the asteroid Gaspra, as well as an unusual asteroid named Ida, which has its own moon, named Dactyl.

The First Mission

NASA's NEAR Shoemaker mission was the first mission to orbit an asteroid. The NEAR Shoemaker probe, launched in February 1996, flew past and took images of Mathilde in 1997, and then entered orbit around Eros in 2000. It studied Eros from orbit for nearly a year, before landing on the asteroid's surface to study it further.

Other Missions

The Japanese Aerospace Exploration Agency (JAXA) launched the Hayabusa probe in 2003. The probe was equipped with a mini-lander called MINERVA, which failed to land on the asteroid's surface. However, samples were collected and analyzed when the probe returned to Earth in 2010. On December 3, 2014, the Hayabusa 2 was launched with the hope it would get samples that could shed light on the origins of the solar system. It entered the orbit of asteroid Ryugu in 2018, where it took samples and even deployed mini rovers to explore further.

This image of the asteroid Ryugu taken by Hayabusa 2 was captured by the probe's Optical Navigation Camera (ONC).

SPACE SCIENCE

The Mariner 9 probe took the first clear images of asteroid-like objects in 1971, 20 years before NEAR Shoemaker. However, the objects it took images of are better known as Deimos and Phobos—the two tiny, lumpy moons that orbit Mars. Most astronomers believe that these moons were originally asteroids that were captured by Mars's gravity. The Voyager probes took images of other solar system moons that are also probably captured asteroids.

NEAR Shoemaker captured stunning images of the planet Mars and its two cratered moons, Phobos and Deimos, shown below right in this image.

Little to Big

The asteroids studied by the early probes were all fairly small. NASA's Dawn probe, launched in 2007, focused on two of the main big hitters of the asteroid belt: Vesta and Ceres. Vesta is 326 miles (525 km) in diameter. Ceres is the biggest object in the asteroid belt, and it is no longer considered to be an asteroid but instead a dwarf planet, in the same category as Pluto.

The Protoplanets

Vesta and Ceres are also considered protoplanets. When the solar system first formed, a huge cloud of dust, gas, and ice swirled around the sun. Eventually the particles started to collide and stick together to form lumps. Once the lumps became big enough, they could attract even more particles with their gravity. They got larger and larger, until they formed protoplanets. Some protoplanets eventually formed planets, and others stayed as they were. A planet's composition changes as it gets bigger, and heavier materials sink into its core. A protoplanet provides a snapshot of what the early solar system was like

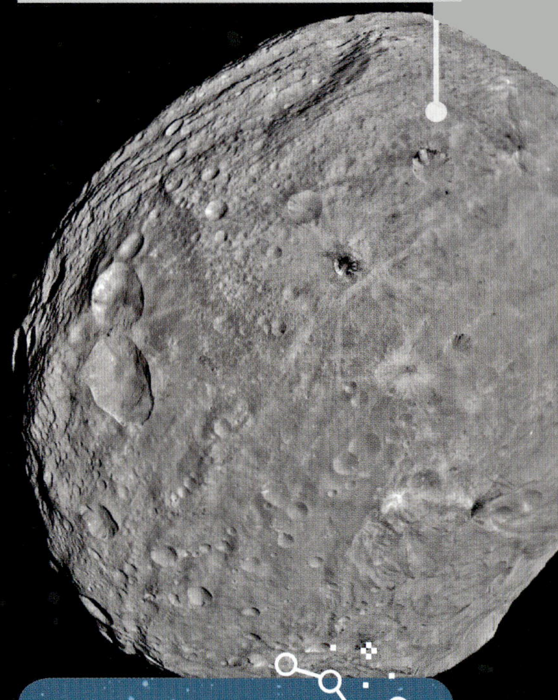

Dawn took this detailed image of the large asteroid Vesta. Craters on its surface show its violent past.

Space Science

Dawn made use of an exciting technology: the ion drive. This type of engine uses charged particles to create thrust. Its fuel is a gas (often xenon), and it needs to carry much less fuel than a conventional rocket engine. The Hayabusa probe also successfully used ion engines.

Dawn in Orbit

Dawn successfully entered orbit around Vesta in 2011. It remained in orbit for about a year, taking images and other readings. It was able to estimate the size of Vesta's core and reveal evidence of ancient asteroid impacts. It then reached Ceres in 2015, and remains in orbit. More missions to asteroids are in the planning stages. Like JAXA's Hayabusa 2 probe, NASA has its own sample return mission, OSIRIS-REx, which took samples from the surface of asteroid Bennu and returned them to Earth in 2023. NASA is also working on a plan to capture a near-Earth asteroid (NEA) and move it into orbit around the moon. It could then be studied in detail by astronauts, and eventually crashed into the moon.

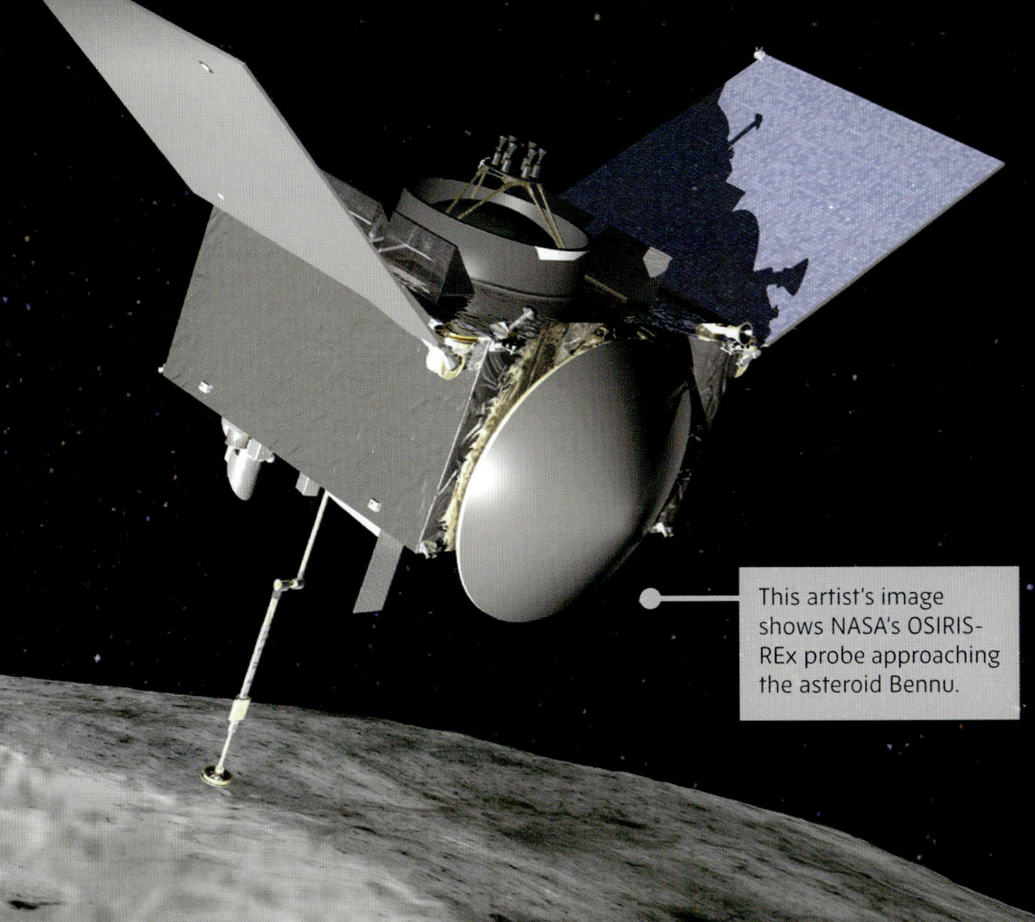

This artist's image shows NASA's OSIRIS-REx probe approaching the asteroid Bennu.

Scarily Close

There are a lot of small asteroids in the solar system that orbit scarily close to Earth. These are known as near-Earth objects (NEOs). You only have to look at the cratered surfaces of the moon or Mercury to know that objects in space have a habit of crashing into each other. We know that at several times in history, large objects have crashed into Earth. For example, many scientists believe that an asteroid 6 miles (9.7 km) across crashed into Earth about 66 million years ago, causing climate changes that contributed to the extinction of the dinosaurs.

Little Asteroid, Big Damage

An asteroid does not have to be very big to cause a lot of damage. In 1908, a huge explosion blasted a remote forest in northern Russia. There was no crater, but for miles around, about 80 million trees were scorched and knocked down. This explosion, now called the Tunguska Event, was felt hundreds of miles away. Many scientists believe that the explosion was caused by an asteroid or comet about 100 feet (30.5 m) across, which exploded before it could impact the ground.

An enormous asteroid crashed into our planet's surface millions of years ago, causing devastation that ended the age of the dinosaurs.

SPACE SCIENCE

Several ideas have been proposed for dealing with an asteroid on a collision course with Earth. One method is to blow it up into smaller pieces, which will either be blown off course or burn up in Earth's atmosphere. Some people have suggested using nuclear weapons to destroy asteroids. Another suggestion is to change the asteroid's course so that it misses Earth. Some scientists have proposed ramming them with a spacecraft or other objects to knock them off course. Another idea is to attach engines to the asteroid, which could "drive" it out of harm's way.

Looking Ahead

Space agencies regularly search for and monitor objects whose orbits take them close to Earth. They focus on those more than 0.6 miles (1 km) in diameter, which would be the most destructive if they crashed into Earth. An impact is unlikely in the near future, but it is best to be prepared!

NEO Surveyor, NASA's next-generation NEO hunter, searches for asteroids that pose a threat to our planet.

YOUR MISSION

How do you think we can protect ourselves against asteroid impacts? Imagine it is your task to plan a strategy to protect Earth from asteroid collisions. In your planning, consider these possible methods:

- Using a missile to destroy an asteroid
- Blowing an asteroid off-course
- Changing an asteroid's course
- Using engines to drive away the asteroid

Of the above, what option do you think is best? Give reasons for your answer.

Chapter 4

STARS THAT FLY

If you look up at the sky on a clear night, you may be lucky enough to see a shooting star, a bright streak of light across the sky. The scientific name for a shooting star is a meteor, and meteors have nothing to do with stars! Little chunks of rock in space are called meteoroids. Occasionally, they get close enough to Earth to enter our atmosphere. When they travel through the atmosphere, it creates friction, which makes the meteoroid so hot that it glows.

Burning Up

Most meteors burn up completely in the atmosphere. However, some make it through and land on Earth. When this happens, they are called meteorites. Over the centuries, people have found meteorites all over Earth. Antarctica is a particularly good place to find them. Ice provides a softer landing than rock, and dark meteorite rocks are easier to spot against a snowy background. Meteorites are a great way for scientists to study what other objects in space are like without ever needing to leave Earth. In many cases, they have been able to tell where a meteorite has come from based on what it is made of.

Fortunately, meteors usually burn up in Earth's atmosphere but some make it to our planet in a spectacular show of light.

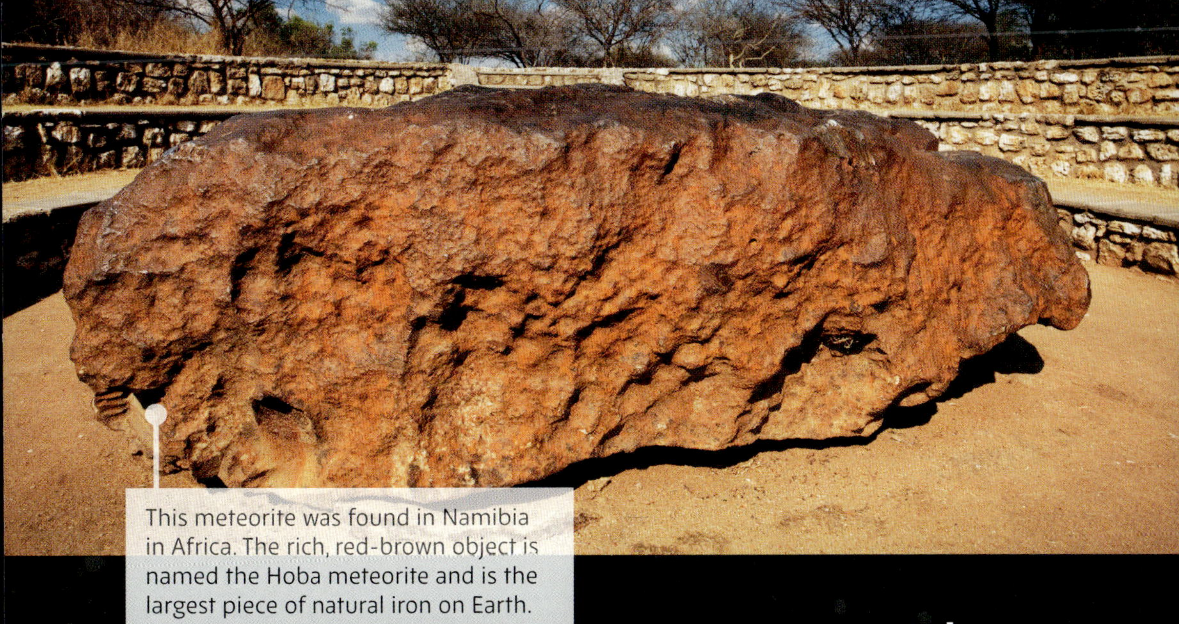

This meteorite was found in Namibia in Africa. The rich, red-brown object is named the Hoba meteorite and is the largest piece of natural iron on Earth.

Too Small for Spacecraft

We do not send spacecraft to visit or investigate meteoroids—they are just too small. They are not big enough to cause large-scale damage, so they are not tracked as asteroids are. However, they are the only type of object from space that regularly turns up practically on our doorstep!

Space Science

You would think that something visible high up in the sky would have to be fairly big, but most meteors are very small. In fact, most of the ones we see are caused by meteoroids smaller than a pebble, and some are as small as a grain of sand. Even these tiny objects can leave a trail several miles long because of their high speed. Meteoroids can enter the atmosphere at anything from 25,000 to 160,000 miles per hour (40,250 to 257,500 kph).

When meteors travel through our planet's atmosphere, they glow brightly with intense heat.

Day or Night

Meteors can appear at any time of day or night, but the meteors that travel near Earth during the day are usually impossible to see, because the sun is so bright. However, sometimes a meteoroid enters Earth's atmosphere and causes a spectacular fireball that is incredibly hard to miss, no matter how bright it may be outside!

Enormous Fireball

One of the most impressive fireballs witnessed in recent years was seen over Chelyabinsk, Russia, on February 15, 2013. A small asteroid estimated to be 65 feet (20 m) wide streaked across the sky, before exploding into thousands of smaller fragments at high altitude. The shock waves from the explosion shattered windows and damaged buildings, causing injuries from broken glass. Many pieces of the meteorite were recovered for study.

SPACE SCIENCE

As a comet travels around the sun, it leaves behind a path of dust and debris. When Earth passes through one of these paths, we get a meteor shower. Tens to hundreds of meteors can be seen each hour. These meteor showers, such as the Perseids and the Leonids, occur at the same time each year.

The Konstantin Kudinov was recorded shooting across the sky above Russia before it smashed into the ground.

The Barringer Crater (also known as Meteor Crater), in Arizona, is believed to have been created about 50,000 years ago by a meteor that measured about 160 feet (49 m) across. Each year, this massive hole in Earth's crust draws thousands of visitors.

When meteor showers such as the Perseids and Leonids are witnessed from Earth they are spectacular to see.

Race Across the Sky

In 1992, thousands of people on the east coast of the United States saw a fireball race across the evening sky. It was a meteorite that eventually landed in Peekskill, New York, on top of a parked car. Many people caught it on film from different locations, and this helped scientists to calculate its flight path.

Everyday Events

Fireballs seem like rare and amazing events, but several thousand probably occur each day. However, most of these happen over the oceans or uninhabited regions. Many also occur during the day, making them harder to see.

Meteorites can be rich in minerals that tell us much about the history of these mysterious rocks.

Space Science

Nearly all meteorites that have been found come from asteroids. However, about 0.2 percent of them come from Mars or the moon. So far scientists have identified nearly 300 meteorites that definitely came from Mars, and they believe the rocks were blasted off the planet's surface by other meteorite impacts. In 2013, data on Mars' atmosphere sent back by the Curiosity rover confirmed that some meteorites really did come from Mars.

Once in a Lifetime

Finding a meteorite may feel like a once-in-a-lifetime event, but meteorites fall to Earth all the time. Scientists estimate that nearly 49 tons (44 mt) of meteorites land on Earth each day! Depending on where they came from, they can be very different in composition. Scientists divide meteorites into three main types: iron, stone, and stony-iron.

Long-Gone Planets

Most iron meteorites are 90 to 95 percent iron, with the remainder made up of nickel and trace elements. They are thought to be the cores of asteroids or long-gone planets. Stony-iron meteorites are made up of equal amounts of nickel-iron and stone. They are believed to have been formed at the core-mantle boundary of an asteroid or planet. Fewer than 2 percent of meteorites are stony-iron. Stony meteorites are the most common. They probably came from the outer crust of other planets and asteroids.

Falling to Earth

The majority of meteorites that fall to Earth are the stone type, but many of the ones we find are irons. One reason for this is that irons are tougher and more likely to survive the fall. Meteorites do not just fall on Earth, either. In 2005, the Mars rover Opportunity found the first-ever meteorite on another planet: a metal meteorite about the size of a basketball. Mars has an extremely thin atmosphere, so meteoroids that hit it do not burn up as much as they do on Earth.

YOUR MISSION

If you were in charge of a mission to study meteorites on Earth, these are some of the tasks that would be involved:

- Choosing an area in which to search for meteorites
- Studying the meteorite
- Collecting samples
- Safely returning the samples to a laboratory
- Studying the samples and analyzing data in the lab

Considering the above, what characteristics and skills would you look for in team members to help you carry out the mission?

Opportunity is equipped with a tool for collecting objects, such as rocks, that it finds on the surface of Mars.

Chapter 5

WHAT ELSE IS OUT THERE?

The solar system is home to an incredible range of bodies, from the tiny grains of rock that cause meteors to the giant gas planets orbiting beyond Mars. However, there are many other types of bodies still to explore. One of the most mysterious of these is the centaurs. These elusive objects are small bodies that orbit the sun, mainly between the orbits of Jupiter and Neptune. Their unstable orbits are affected by the gravity of the gas giants, and they sometimes cross the planets' orbits.

Finding the First Centaur

The first centaur, Chiron, was discovered in 1977, and the second, Pholus, in 1992. Since then, hundreds of others have been reported, and astronomers believe that many more are yet to be found. They range in size from tens of miles to about 160 miles (257.5 km) in diameter, which is much larger than most comets. Astronomers believe most centaurs only spend a relatively short time as centaurs. They will eventually collide with a planet or be thrown by a planet's gravity either toward the sun or out of the solar system.

C/2014 Q2 Lovejoy is a fascinating long-period comet that was discovered in 2014 by the astronomer Terry Lovejoy. The comet journeys so far out in our solar system that it takes 19,000 years to orbit the sun.

Scientists are constantly learning more about asteroids and other intriguing objects that travel through space.

Inside or Outside the Solar System?

Some astronomers thought centaurs were asteroids flung out from the inner solar system. Others thought they were comets on their way in from the outer solar system. In 2013, data from NASA's WISE telescope suggested that about two-thirds of centaurs are actually comets. It studied the objects' reflectivity and discovered that most of them are dark, like comets. This means they are probably made from the same materials as a comet. They may have been active comets in the past, and they may be active again one day.

SPACE HISTORY

In Greek mythology, centaurs were creatures that had the legs and body of a horse, but the head and torso of a human. Centaurs in space also seem to be half one thing and half another. In some ways, they are like asteroids, but in other ways they are more similar to comets.

Discovering Dwarf Planets

Astronomy is exciting because new developments and discoveries are made all the time. As technology improves, we learn more about the solar system and the rest of space. Sometimes what we find makes us reevaluate what we thought we knew. This is why, in 2006, the International Astronomical Union (IAU) adopted a brand new class of space objects: the dwarf planet.

Finding Pluto

Pluto was discovered in 1930, becoming the ninth planet of the solar system. As astronomers learned more about it, it began to seem like the odd one out among the planets. It was tiny, with an unusual orbit, and was icier than the other rocky planets. In the 1990s, astronomers started finding more objects in the same region of space as Pluto, or even farther away.

This image shows Pluto (above) and Charon (upper left). It was taken by NASA's New Horizons spacecraft.

New Planets Too?

By 2005, there were three objects (Quaoar, Eris, and Sedna) that were of a similar size to Pluto. This left astronomers with a problem: were these new objects also planets? It was quite likely that several more similar objects were still to be found. How many planets would we end up with? If they were not planets, then where did that leave Pluto?

Like Pluto, Quaoar is in the Kuiper Belt, an icy-cold area filled with comet-like objects.

Big Debates

After a lot of debate, the IAU adopted a new definition of a planet, and created a new category for dwarf planets. Pluto is now called a dwarf planet, along with Ceres, Haumea, Makemake, and Eris. All of these except for Ceres, which is in the asteroid belt, are found in the outer solar system. Several other objects in this area appear to have the characteristics of dwarf planets. These include Quaoar, Sedna, Salacia, and Orcus.

SPACE SCIENCE

Since 2006, the IAU's definition of a planet is that it must orbit the sun, be massive enough to have a nearly round shape, and it must have "cleared the neighborhood" around its orbit. This last requirement means that a planet must be massive enough for its gravity to have removed any smaller rocky or icy objects from its orbit. Objects that meet the first two criteria, but not the third, are now known as dwarf planets.

Far from the Sun

Although Pluto is a long way from the sun, it has a lot of company in the space beyond the orbit of Neptune. It is part of the Kuiper Belt. This part of space contains many icy bodies other than Pluto. Astronomers estimate that there are hundreds of millions of objects in the Kuiper Belt, most of them are left over from the formation of the outer planets.

A New Idea

In the 1950s, the Dutch astronomer Jan Oort (1900–1992) had proposed the existence of a giant spherical cloud of icy bodies, where long-period comets came from. This area is now known as the Oort Cloud. However, another astronomer, Gerard Kuiper (1905–1973), soon realized that short-period comets must come from somewhere closer than the Oort Cloud. He suggested that there was a flattened ring of objects outside the orbit of Neptune. His theory was widely accepted, but it was only in the 1990s that telescopes became powerful and sensitive enough to detect the Kuiper Belt.

Space Science

In early 2006, when Pluto was still considered to be a planet, the New Horizons spacecraft blasted off from Cape Canaveral in Florida. It flew by Pluto and its moons in 2015, the first spacecraft to visit the dwarf planet. New Horizons also visited the KBO Arrokoth on 1 January 2019.

This is an artist's image of the Kuiper Belt object 2003 UB313, which is nicknamed Xena.

First Finds

The first KBO was detected in 1992. Others soon followed, and within 20 years about 1,500 had been identified. Most of the objects that have been detected are fairly large, with diameters between 300 and 1,000 miles (482 and 1,600 km). However, there are likely to be many smaller objects too difficult to make out from Earth. Some of the largest KBOs, including Eris and Pluto, have their own moons. Most KBOs are made mainly of ice containing methane, ammonia, and water. The ice would vaporize if a KBO traveled on a path toward the sun and warmed up, forming a coma and tail.

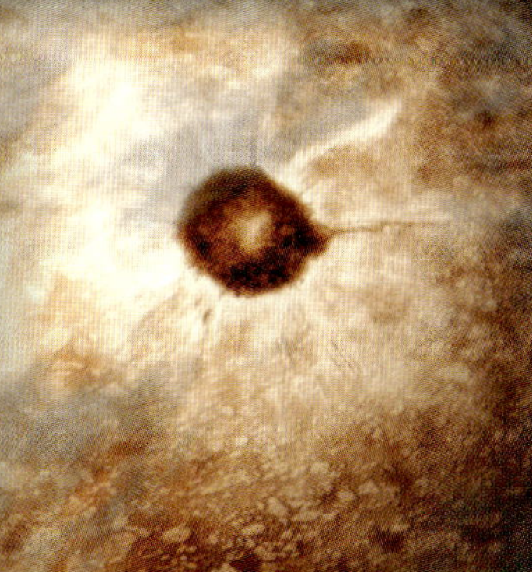

New Horizons gathered extraordinary information about Pluto and its moon Charon as it flew past the mysterious bodies.

YOUR MISSION

Imagine it is your task to plan a spacecraft for a manned mission beyond the Kuiper Belt. In your planning, consider:

- Onboard workspace: what equipment would be needed? What type of space would be most effective for study and work?
- Onboard living space: what would you need to provide for the crew?

Try to consider all aspects of human health in your planning, both mental and physical. They are equally important for a healthy crew.

Chapter 6

ALWAYS MORE MISSIONS

There are many reasons for studying smaller solar system bodies such as asteroids, comets, and dwarf planets. They can tell us a lot about how the solar system was formed, and give us clues to the early days of Earth. Asteroids are debris left over from the very early days of the solar system, when the planets were first forming. Their composition can teach us about the elements involved in the chemical mixture that formed Earth.

Countless Collisions

Asteroids and comets have collided with Earth countless times in the past, and will likely do so again in the future. Finding and tracking objects in space that could one day crash into our planet is an extremely important job. With enough warning, we may be able to take steps to avoid a collision. The more we know about their composition and movement through space, the better prepared we can be.

The National Observatory of Athens, Greece, was built in 1842. It is one of the oldest space research centers in the world.

Early asteroids that hit our planet may have brought more than destruction, including factors that helped life flourish.

Catastrophe on Earth

In the past, collisions have sometimes had catastrophic effects for life on Earth, but even farther back, they may have helped to create it. Many astronomers believe that the water and organic molecules necessary for life to begin may have arrived on our planet when comets or asteroids crashed into it. Learning more about comets and asteroids could help solve the mystery of how life evolved on Earth.

Could Be Useful?

Studying asteroids could help identify which ones contain useful materials. Some asteroids are known to contain water, precious metals, and other elements, all of which can be sent to Earth, or could be used by people on space missions. The asteroids themselves could also be useful as bases for further space exploration.

SPACE SCIENCE

In movies, the asteroid belt is usually shown as being full of rocks, with spacecraft swerving to avoid collisions. Unfortunately, the reality is far less exciting! As a very rough average, there is about one asteroid within an area the size of Rhode Island. A patch of the asteroid belt the size of the entire United States would have only about 2,000 asteroids. If you were standing on an asteroid, the nearest 0.6-mile (1 km) across asteroid would probably be impossible to see without a telescope.

Where Did We Come From?

When Earth first formed about 4.5 billion years ago, it was a very different place from the planet we know now. Its hot surface was constantly changing due to volcanic activity and impacts from meteorites. Eventually things cooled down a little, the surface solidified, and oceans covered much of Earth. At some point about 3.8 billion years ago, the first life appeared on Earth in the form of single-celled organisms, such as bacteria.

Tiniest of All Life

The tiniest unit of life is the cell, and cells themselves are made up of atoms and molecules of a range of different elements. Many scientists believe that living things developed from molecules that could replicate, or make copies of, themselves. Eventually these molecules joined with others, becoming more and more complex. Through the process of evolution, they developed into the wide range of living things we know today.

Today, our planet is filled with life and covered largely with water. However, long ago it was a violently hot and unstable place.

Our solar system has a dramatic past, filled with collisions between asteroids and protoplanets.

More Debate

How those first molecules came about is a subject of much debate. For example, one theory concerns amino acids, some of the building blocks of life. In the 1950s, scientists showed that amino acids could have formed naturally in the early Earth's atmosphere. The necessary raw materials were present, and by using electric sparks to simulate lightning strikes they were able to create amino acids. However, other scientists believe that the building blocks of life could have come from elsewhere in the solar system, brought here on one of the comets or asteroids that crashed into the planet. New discoveries about these objects bring us closer to discovering the truth.

Space Science

During the period when Earth was bombarded by asteroids and comets, it would have been extremely hot, and the oceans would have vaporized. So where did our planet get all its water? One theory is that it came from comets, which are mainly made of ice. Not all comets have the same type of water that is found here on Earth, but in 2011, the ESA's Herschel Space Telescope detected signs of Earth ocean-type water in Comet Hartley 2.

Using Asteroids

Many of Earth's natural resources are finite. We are using up the available supplies of oil, natural gas, helium, and many other substances. Amazingly, the solution may lie in space: in the near future, we may be able to mine asteroids. Astronomers are already able to use spectroscopy, which analyzes the light reflected from an asteroid, to find out what substances it contains. Scientists know that many asteroids contain iron, nickel, and magnesium. Some could also contain water, oxygen, gold, and platinum.

Rather than bringing destruction, could the asteroids in our solar system instead provide us with rich and valuable resources?

Study and Support

There are two main reasons for mining asteroids. The first would be to send valuable materials, such as gold and platinum, back to Earth. A second reason would be to extract materials that could help support the astronauts doing the mining, as well as colonies elsewhere in the solar system. For example, extracting water ice would yield water that colonists could use for drinking and growing food, and it could also be broken down into hydrogen and oxygen to make rocket fuel. Even the high cost of setting up a mine on an asteroid would probably still be cheaper than sending the same materials from Earth to the moon or Mars.

Asteroids such as Psyche contain many valuable minerals. The hope is that one day we may be able to harvest and use these resources.

A Mining Mission

An asteroid-mining operation would probably rely heavily on robots, and most machines would be solar or nuclear powered. Since asteroids have very little gravity, the astronauts and the mining equipment would have to be anchored to the surface somehow. It would be a huge challenge; but it could really be worth it: one NASA report estimates that the total amount of minerals found in the asteroid belt would be worth the equivalent of $100 billion for each person on Earth!

This is an artist's impression of a method we could one day use to mine the minerals in asteroids.

SPACE SCIENCE

Some of the minerals that we already mine from Earth's crust, such as cobalt, platinum, and tungsten, may have originally come from asteroids that collided with Earth. When Earth first formed, it pulled these heavier elements out of the crust and into its core. Scientists believe that asteroids crashing into Earth's crust brought new supplies of these heavy metals.

YOUR MISSION

Imagine it is your mission to write a report analyzing the benefits of a mining expedition to an asteroid. Investors in the project are concerned about risks and hazards, including the below:

- Danger to the crew
- Costs of the mission
- Environmental issues if mined materials returned to Earth contain dangerous components

How would you persuade them that the benefits of the expedition outweigh any disadvantages? Give reasons for your answers.

CONCLUSION

FUTURE MISSIONS

In the past 50 years, we have learned a huge amount about asteroids, comets, and other small bodies in space. Space agencies such as NASA, ESA, and JAXA are working on future missions to learn more about asteroids and comets. Private companies are getting in on the action, too. The company SpaceX recently provided the rocket to launch NASA's mission to explore the metal-rich asteroid Psyche.

Astronauts to an NEA

One proposed mission would send astronauts to visit an NEA. It would be a challenging and dangerous mission lasting about six months. The astronauts would be traveling beyond the safety of Earth's magnetic field, leaving them exposed to strong radiation. They would also be too far from Earth for rescue, if anything went wrong during the mission.

Scientists hope that Psyche will be one of the first rockets to power missions to mine the riches of our solar system.

Using Robots

However, one safer option for studying asteroids up close would be to use a robotic spacecraft to drag a small asteroid into orbit around the moon. From there, it would be easier to study or mine. NASA scientists believe that such a mission would be possible in the near future. One plan would use a slow-moving spacecraft with a large bag to catch an asteroid about 20 feet (6 m) across, then drag the asteroid back to the moon.

Already Underway

Other missions are already in progress. NASA's OSIRIS-REx spacecraft is on its way to study another asteroid now that it has returned its samples of the asteroid Bennu to Earth. Scientists are studying the samples with the hope that the material will provide clues to the origin of life on Earth, and also the possibility of life elsewhere in the solar system.

YOUR FUTURE MISSION

Perhaps this book has inspired you to find out more about comets, asteroids, and other space bodies. Maybe, one day, you'll even carve out a career in space science and make it your mission to explore the mysteries of the universe and unlock its secrets.

GLOSSARY

amino acids organic chemicals necessary to build proteins

asteroids small, rocky, planet-like bodies that orbit the sun but are not big enough to be considered planets

atmosphere the layer of gases surrounding a planet or moon

atoms the smallest possible units of a chemical element. Atoms are the basis of all matter in the universe

cell the smallest unit of life

centaurs small objects in the solar system that have some characteristics of comets and some characteristics of asteroids

coma the glowing cloud that surrounds the nucleus of a comet when it is close to the sun

comets icy objects in space that travel in long, looping paths around the sun

crater a hollow area, like the inside of a bowl, created when an object crashes into a planet or other large object

crust the hard outer shell of something

dwarf planet an object in the solar system that has not cleared out its own orbit of other major bodies in order to be considered a planet

fireball a very bright meteor

galaxies groups of hundreds of billions of stars and other matter held together by gravity

gravity the force that pulls all objects toward each other

infrared a type of electromagnetic energy with a long wavelength, which cannot be seen as visible light

ion drive a type of engine that uses charged particles to provide thrust

mantle the part of a planet, asteroid, or comet that lies between the crust and central core

meteorites lumps of stone or metal from a meteor that has landed on Earth

meteoroids small lumps of rock or other matter that travel through the solar system

meteors the bright streaks in the sky seen when meteoroids travel through Earth's atmosphere

meteor shower an event in which many meteors appear in the sky, appearing to come from the same source

molecules the smallest units of substances that have all the properties of those substances. Molecules are made up of atoms

natural resources materials that are found in nature and that can be used by people in many ways

nucleus the central part of a comet, which vaporizes when it nears the sun to produce a coma and tail

orbiting when one body in space travels on a curved path around another object, such as a moon orbiting a planet

probe an instrument or tool used to explore something that cannot be observed directly

protoplanets objects in space that are planets in their early stages of evolution

rotated spun around a central axis. The rotation of Earth is what causes night and day

trojans rocky objects in space that share the orbit of a much larger object, such as a planet

vaporize to turn into gas

BOOKS

Barr, Catherine. *The Universe and Its Mysteries* (Space Voyage). Rosen Publishing Group, 2022.

Harman, Alice. *Asteroids and Comets* (Fact Frenzy). Rosen Publishing Group, 2021.

Hubbard, Ben. *The Complete Guide to Space Exploration: A Journey of Discovery Across the Universe*. Lonely Planet Kids, 2020.

WEBSITES

Learn more about asteroids at:
kids.britannica.com/students/article/asteroid/272984

Find out more about meteors at:
kids.britannica.com/students/article/meteor-and-meteorite/275807

Discover more about asteroids at:
www.nationalgeographic.co.uk/search?q=asteroids

Publisher's note to educators and parents:
All the websites featured above have been carefully reviewed to ensure that they are suitable for students. However, many websites change often, and we cannot guarantee that a site's future contents will continue to meet our high standards of educational value. Please be advised that students should be closely monitored whenever they access the Internet.

INDEX

ABOUT THE AUTHOR

Sarah Eason has written many children's books and has a particular interest in space science. She has found researching and writing this book fascinating and hopes that it helps readers better understand the mysteries of space and maybe make it their mission to become a future space explorer.